Spiral
of Violence

Helder Camara

translated by Della Couling

Sheed and Ward · London and Sydney

First published 1971
Sheed and Ward Ltd, 33 Maiden Lane, London WC2E 7LA
and
Sheed and Ward Pty Ltd,
204 Clarence Street, Sydney, NSW 2000

Originally published as *Spirale de Violence*
by Desclée de Broucker, Brussels 1970

Nihil obstat : John M. T. Barton, STD, LSS
Imprimatur : + Victor Guazelli, VG
Westminster, 7 December 1970

The Nihil obstat and Imprimatur are a declaration that a
book or pamphlet is considered to be free from doctrinal
or moral error. It is not implied that those who have
granted the Nihil obstat and Imprimatur agree with the
contents, opinions, or statements expressed.

ISBN 0 7220 0624 1
This book is set in 12/13½ pt Linotype Baskerville
Made and printed in Great Britain by
William Clowes and Sons Ltd, London, Beccles
and Colchester

To the memory of
Gandhi and Martin Luther King

Contents

Introduction
Brian Darling

Who is Helder Camara? To those of us who have had the experience of meeting him, or of hearing him address a meeting, or simply of trying to follow his itinerary of thought and of action, this might seem an offensive—certainly unnecessary question. But it is one that can, and must be answered, initially at least, in two different ways. We can first think of him as a man of the church and trace his career from seminary to the Archbishopric of Olinda and Recife in North-East Brazil, we can add that he has shown himself to be a formidable organiser of churchmen, making them a force to be reckoned with in contemporary Latin America.

1

Alternatively we could say that he is a man who is accused by his government and large sections of Brazilian society of being a communist subversive, of travelling round the world leading a smear campaign against his government. A man who is under constant threat of assassination by other 'christians' but refuses any bodyguard or even a lock on his door.

Each answer, sufficiently developed, would show us a remarkable man. But neither would go far enough to enable us to understand the complexity and heroism of this violent peacemaker, or to grasp the panic which clearly seized the Brazilian government as, during 1970, a succession of important groups and individuals declared their support for the candidature of Dom Helder for the Nobel Peace Prize. Instead we need to combine the two approaches and place the man's biography and ideas in the context of his society and the wider world.

Dom Helder—the man of the church

Helder was born in that *nordeste* to which he was later to return in February 1909, in

Fortaleza, capital of the State of Ceara. His mother was a teacher in a government primary school and his father a journalist and theatre critic. Looking back we can see that much of the style of Dom Helder the world figure is contained in the vocations of his parents. But this is to anticipate . . .

After training at the seminary, where his qualities and energy were already to make him a controversial student, the future archbishop was ordained priest in 1931. By 1934 he had already been appointed Secretary for Education in his home state of Ceara, and in 1936 went to Rio de Janeiro where he was to pass the next twenty-eight years. During all this time Helder was to occupy increasingly important posts in the educational establishment of Brazil and by the time he left Rio to return to the *nordeste* in 1964 he was a member of the Supreme Council for Education. Parallel to his work in education Dom Helder started to take an interest in the organisation of the Brazilian church and was particularly concerned to find a way of getting bishops better informed about the realities of the problems of their country and better equipped to act as a body.

The fruits of this more or less single-handed struggle are to be seen in the Conference of Brazilian Bishops, collegiate authority of the church in Brazil (Dom Helder was its Secretary General for twelve years), and in CELAM, the Latin American Episcopal Council, whose meeting at Medellin (Colombia) in 1968 was to prove a turning point in the long history of the Catholic Church in Latin America. It would be no exaggeration to say that the image of Camilo Torres dominated Medellin in a way analogous to that of the absent Ernesto Che Guevara at the conference of the Organisation for Latin American Solidarity in Havana the previous year.

The first meeting of CELAM took place in 1955, a busy year for Dom Helder. With some years' experience of organising the Brazilian Bishops' Conference behind him, he was named auxiliary bishop by Cardinal Jaime de Barros Camara of Rio (no relation), and, in addition, he organised the International Eucharistic Congress in Rio. It was this congress which marked a turning point in Dom Helder's already very active life. After the meeting had ended its organiser received a private visit from Cardinal Gerlier of Lyon. Gerlier observed that the congress had been remarkably well organised and then went on to suggest that these talents which Dom Helder so clearly had would be better used to solve the problems of the *favelas*, those festering piles of human beings separated by bits of cardboard and corrugated iron which grotesquely command the finest view of the most beautiful bay in the world. In eight years of deeper and deeper involvement Dom Helder was to get to a point where his cardinal asked the Vatican to remove him to a less embarrassing spot.

Dom Helder—the political figure

By his own admission[1] Helder was, in his youth, tempted by the Brazilian version of

[1] This and many other details of Dom Helder's life, and quotations, are taken from the excellent biography by José de Broucker, *Dom Helder Camara: la violence d'un pacifique*, Paris, Fayard, 1969. All translations from this are my own. There is an English translation. *The Violence of*

fascism, 'integrism'. For two years he was in the movement, where everyone talked about God, the Fatherland and the Family. The inspiration was Salazar rather than Hitler or Mussolini and the simple idea that 'order' was more important than 'justice'. Dom Helder's critics have made much of this flirtation as an attempt to discredit the archbishop in the eyes of the liberal and progressive forces who support his present work. The important thing of course is that in thirty-five years Dom Helder's position has changed radically. And it is precisely because Brazilian society is taking the opposite direction and has moved from a preoccupation with justice to an obsession with order that Dom Helder's work, which elsewhere would be seen as no more dramatic than that of a Bishop Huddleston in Tanzania, takes on heroic dimensions.

The years of Helder Camara's increasing involvement in the problems of the *favelas* of Rio were also decisive years in Brazilian history. This is not the place to write a his-

---

a Peacemaker: Dom Helder Camara, published by Orbis Books, Maryknoll, New York.

tory of the period, but a rough sketch of some of the background is necessary at this point.

Brazil is by far the largest country of Latin America, is larger than Europe and as big as the United States without Alaska. It is already the most industrialised but is also potentially the richest and most powerful country south of the rio Grande.

However, if Brazil has, as it does in certain areas of Rio and São Paulo, oases of the most modern affluent society, these must be seen in a functional relationship to the extremes of poverty in the *favelas* and to the archaic structures of most of the rural sector of the economy. In Brazil, according to the most recent official figures,[2] 28 per cent of the national income goes to about 900,000 people (one per cent of the population) while about the same fraction (35 per cent) of the national income is shared by 72,000,000 people (80 per cent of the population). Similarly, 80 per cent of

[2] Cf *Correio da Manha*, Rio de Janeiro, 31 May 1970, reporting on studies by the UN Commission for Latin America.

cultivated land belongs to 2 per cent of landowners. Only 3 per cent of the land surface is cultivated. Such statistics, eloquent though they are in expressing fundamental inequalities, nevertheless hide certain crucial sociological realities.

The first of these is the form of economic conditions which exist in the agricultural sector, ranging from wage-earning through forms of indenture to virtual slavery. And alongside this the forms of political control which the landowners continue to exercise over the illiterate, diseased and starving peasants.

Another crucial point is the ultra-rapid growth of the big cities, particularly in the South Central region. Unfortunately the latest figures we have are already ten years old, but even these tell us a lot. In 1920 less than 4 per cent of the population lived in towns of over half a million inhabitants; by 1960 it was nearly 13 per cent of a population that had more than doubled. The source of these new urban populations is two-fold, migration from the countryside and migration from abroad, particularly

Europe, and as many studies[3] have shown, the origins of these new migrants and their new situation in an expanding inflationary economy made for an ideology of individual upward social mobility. This meant that, though the industrial workers might be organised in strong trade unions, it was always possible to buy off militancy with welfare policies. As a result, the emergence of an urban working class in Brazil did not significantly change the workings of the political system which was based upon the skilful manipulation of socio-economic, regional, military, religious and, most important, international, interest groups. But by the late fifties and early sixties certain external factors were to have profound repercussions in Brazil, and throughout Latin America, the Cuban revolution and the papal encyclicals. The extent of the influence of the Cuban example elsewhere in the sub-continent is still the subject for

[3] Most easily accessible is the essay by Celso Furtado, 'Political Obstacles to Economic Growth in Brazil', in Claudio Veliz (ed.), *Obstacles to Change in Latin America*, Oxford University Press, 1965.

much debate, but there is a minimum area of agreement to the effect that it strengthened the will of certain groups to throw off the Yanqui yoke and particularly showed the revolutionary potential of the peasantry. The papal encyclicals of John XXIII and Paul VI have noticeably strengthened the hand of the socially concerned wing of the church in Latin America, and made the dialogue with secular political groups of the left much more meaningful.

These external factors then, allied to the industrial sector's growing need for a less archaic agricultural partner in the process of capital formation, led to a race for the allegiance of the peasants. Everyone was in favour of development, at least in theory, but was it to be capitalism or socialism? Was it to be an authentic Brazilian development or merely accession to the status of junior partner to the United States of America? To the former question the encyclicals' reply seemed not to be an unequivocal condemnation of socialism provided it was not 'atheistic communism'. And on the second, well surely if little Cuba could resist the Yanqui, then Brazil....

The questions were being posed with particular force in Dom Helder's native *nordeste*. It was here that Francisco Juliao, a lawyer, set about organising peasant leagues (*ligas camponesas*) which demanded social ownership of land rather than the reforms within the framework of a system of private property which the advanced sectors of the urban industrial bourgeoisie were advocating. It was principally in the *nordeste* that the literacy campaigns based on the primer of Paolo Freire 'Viver è lutar' (To live is to struggle), were conducted by a young and dynamic Basic Education Movement (MEB), supported by regular radio programmes sponsored by the Bishops' Conference. In 1963 MEB was operating in twelve states; 7,500 instructors plus 180,000 pupils plus 15,000 transistor radios. It was a recipe for dynamite. Along with the basic skills of literacy the peasants were introduced to the concepts of justice and exploitation, dignity and action.[4] It was to the *nordeste* that idealistic young technocrats came to work at the SUDENE, an or-

[4] Cf E. de Kadt, *Catholic Radicals in Brazil*, Oxford University Press, 1970.

ganisation which was going to supervise the rational exploitation of the resources of the region. And it was in the State of Pernambuco that Governor Miguel Arraes was putting into practice his form of participatory democracy where the governor and his ministers would go out to the people and discuss, with local leaders or with assemblies of whole populations in the town or village centres, the economic and social policies of the state, the constraints they were operating under, both national and international. This was the political keystone of a whole edifice which comprised the literary campaigns, the popular culture movement, the SUDENE, etc., and not surprisingly it reverberated throughout Brazil.

This experience in Recife led to rising expectations of a real democratisation, but the political structures of the country did not permit this. Janio Quadros, who had been elected president in 1961, attempted to establish an independent foreign policy and end corruption, particularly in the civil service, where he ordered employees to work full office hours in place of their current practice of working half-time and taking a second job.

Quadros was forced to resign after a few months, and the succession of the vice-president, Joao Goulart, was blocked by the army until a compromise could be reached which transferred important powers from the president to a parliament dominated by traditional interests. A referendum was needed to restore the presidential powers, which left Goulart with debts to pay to the unions and other supporters. In early 1964, in the face of 100% inflation, he doubled public sector salaries overnight. But this was the improvisation of a traditional politician without much conviction and when the alliance of large landowners, urban middle-classes, armed forces and the United States decided that that was enough, in went the tanks. It would be easy to say, as was the aim of the authors of the coup of 1 April 1964, that the tanks pushed over the fragile edifice which was the democracy of the *nordeste*. True they arrested and imprisoned Arraes, Juliao, dozens of officials of the movements and hundreds of anonymous peasants, trade unionists and students.

The movements were dissolved, the SUDENE headed by an army officer. But the point about that 'democratic dawn' is that it succeeded in changing consciousness, and even tanks and torture cannot crush that advance.

It was into this new setting that Helder Camara came in April 1964 as Archbishop of Olinda and Recife. His message to the people of his diocese upon taking possession is characteristic both in its simplicity and its announcement of positions that will be defended: 'Let us not think that the problem is limited to certain slight reforms and let us not confuse the good and indispensable notion of order, the goal of all human progress, with caricatures of it which are responsible for the persistence of structures which everyone recognises cannot be preserved.'[5]

Dom Helder—the world figure

Though he was an energetic bishop in his

[5] Helder Camara, *Church and Colonialism*, London, Sheed and Ward, and Denville, NJ, Dimension Books, 1969, p. 6.

nordeste and an untiring traveller and speaker pleading the cause of the peoples of the Third World, it is not until 1968 that Helder Camara really becomes a world figure and a symbol. 1968 is thought of in Europe as the year of Paris and Prague; in Brazil it marks the passage to a higher form of repression in the form of the Institutional Act No 5 in which habeas corpus and the few remaining legal guarantees were abolished. In addition the new president General Garrastazu Medici, ex-chief of the secret services, vested himself with the right to cancel the mandate of any parliamentary representative without any form of trial and to suspend the political rights of any citizens. By 1 September 1970 more than 5,000 Brazilian citizens had lost their rights because of opposition to the regime. Under the National Security Law, promulgated by the regime, all citizens are now placed under military justice.

Such legislation has left the church in Brazil as the only public structured organisation not directly controlled by the dictatorship. The growth of arbitrary rule and the widespread use of torture as an instrument of policy have presented a moral problem for the whole church, but it has become a practical problem too, especially for those whose work brings them into direct contact with the more obvious victims of the repressions. Do they betray their people by keeping quiet or do they stand up and denounce injustice only to take the supreme punishment? The supreme punishment, what can this be for a priest, death . . . or suicide?

In Brazil this is not a question for academic theologians. They have concrete examples and for brevity I will give just one of each. In April of 1969 while Dom Helder was visiting England to address a number of meetings of young people he was treated as a 'star' by the English press. Here at last was authentic christianity defining itself in adversity, the 'puckish' smile as the *Times* put it. Then Dom Helder returned to Brazil and there was silence. No-one seemed concerned that he was now back in this arbitrary society he had so simply and eloquently denounced. Less than a month later it was learned that one of his principal collaborators, Father Antonio Henrique

Pereira Neto, had been barbarously assassinated in Recife (amongst other things he was tied up, dragged along the ground, shot three times in the head, and hung by the neck from a tree). His crime? To have been chaplain to the students of the University of Recife. His assassins have not yet been found.

Or take the case of Father Tito de Alencar OP who is being tried, along with six other Dominicans, by the second military tribunal of São Paulo at the time I write these lines. I shall return to their trial later since it indicates a very important development in the relations between church and state, but for the moment let us return to Fr Tito's calvary:[6]

> . . . I persisted in denying, and they continued to give me electric shocks, kicks, blows with a rod and punches in the ribs. Once Captain Albernaz had me open my mouth to 'receive the sacrament of the eucharist'. They put in an electric wire. . . .

[6] Fr Tito's letter was reprinted in *New Blackfriars*, July 1970.

After a detailed account of the tortures he endured, Tito tells how he came to the supreme decision to commit suicide—'. . . in my case it was a question of preventing others from being tortured and of denouncing before public opinion and before the church what goes on in the prisons of Brazil. I was convinced that this could not be done without sacrificing my life.' Fortunately he was too public a figure to lose if he could be saved and his death in prison might embarrass the regime. In a critical state as a result of loss of blood he was taken to hospital where instead they tried to convince him that he was mad.

Two cases among hundreds, but there are two general points to be underlined: There are presently more than 12,000 political prisoners in Brazil and, according to the report made by representatives of Amnesty International, the average age of these prisoners is twenty-two years. As the representatives of Catholic youth movements have put it, 'It is a crime to be young today in Brazil.' The second point is made for us by Fr Tito, 'The hope of these political prisoners is based on the church, the only institution in Brazil not under control of the Military State.'

Dom Helder clearly understands this when he says to his biographer:

> And so for the moment—I can say this to you and other Europeans especially—I am making the most of a certain clerical advantage. There! That is what I am doing! Because, in this country today and in present conditions, a bishop can say what a student or workman or an intellectual, even a professor, could not risk saying.

This duty to resist is by no means felt by all members of the church hierarchy and the dictatorship seems to have little difficulty in finding an eminent member of the church to insist that there are no political prisoners and there is no torture, etc. But the cat is out of the bag now.

Nevertheless the charges of 'communism' and 'subversion' are still made against all who resist the regime's juggernaut, and the armed forces seem impervious to Dom

Helder's logic:

Paul VI was right to say, 'The earth was given to us all, not just to the rich.'

No-one thinks that is communism: it is the voice of the Pope.

Private property, yes, if it is for all.

But not private property which deprives. . . .

In fact, of course, Helder Camara's politics derive very clearly from conventional Catholic 'social teaching'; what makes the difference is that he applies them to a very unconventional situation—and, one might add, in a very unconventional way. He is constantly quoting from encyclicals, especially *Populorum Progressio*, but this orthodoxy takes on revolutionary implications in the context of contemporary Brazilian politics. To return to the trial of the Dominicans, amongst the charges laid against them is one that accuses them of 'disobeying the teaching of the popes (Leo XII, Pius X, Pius XI and Pius XII) in accepting communism which these popes had expressly condemned'. They are also accused by the Military Prosecutor of quoting to justify their actions '*Mater et Magistra, Pacem in*

Terris, Populorum Progressio, and the official documents (from the CEPAL conference at Medellin) of the Bishops of Brazil and of Latin America'. Indeed to defend the pope has become a hazardous occupation nowadays. Dom Sigaud, Archbishop of Diamantina, recently in Europe to denounce Dom Helder, gained a certain notoriety at the second Vatican Council by his attacks on John XXIII ('influenced by the communists') and on Paul VI, who was 'suffering from complexes because his family had been persecuted by the fascists'.

Far from being a promoter of dangerously new ideas, Dom Helder is firmly within the mainstream of catholicism, indeed, one reason for his growing influence within the church is that he typifies the renewal of the church called for by the Vatican Council. He has not joined in the controversies over celibacy or church government, largely, it seems, because he regards them as a distraction from more important work. It is important for him to move with the church (and so move the church), and to this end he uses his considerable diplomatic talents. This is the significance of his work in building up CELAM and the Brazilian Bishops' Conference, long before the Vatican Council recommended such coordination for the whole church. Similarly, he has made no speeches about celibacy but makes no secret of his attitude to those of his own priests who have married or left the ministry: 'They stay in touch with us. They are friends, not enemies. We work together.' It is part of the same pattern that he should be both a supporter of the pope and a friend of Cardinal Suenens, a leading critic of overcentralised church government. Of Suenens he has said, 'When I look at him, I say to myself that he is somehow our leader, the leader of all those who want to make Vatican II a living reality.'

His politics too are essentially practical and empirical; his non-violence is not a condemnation of violence but an insistence that for 'his' people violence would be suicide. 'I respect and shall always respect those who, after thinking about it, have chosen or will choose violence.' Certainly he would agree with his close friend Alceu Amoroso Lima when he describes Camilo

Torres as a 'martyr for the Christ of to-morrow'.[7]

Dom Helder Camara is more a prophet than either a politician or theologian. He is a simple man, simple in his way of life, in his way with people—simple as a prophet should be. But as Brazil is the land of contrasts—São Paulo *and* the *sertão*, so this prophet comes in from the deserts from time to time and enters the world of McLuhan. There one finds the Dom Helder of the theatre, the son of the theatre critic, the little boy who spent hours in wonderment watching rehearsals. There is an element of the simple child in the Dom Helder we see in Europe—in Manchester, at the Roundhouse, in Paris at the Palais des Sports or the Mutualité. The wide gestures, the simple soutane, the simple smile—always the same term comes back, simplicity. But this is not the simple man. This is the prophet from modern Brazil and the man of the theatre who knows how to launch a manifesto.

De Broncker captures this exactly:

[7] Quoted in Alain Gheerbrant, *L'Eglise rebelle d'Amérique Latine*, Paris, Seuil, 1969.

He had booked a small hall that could take about three or four hundred people from the nuns who run the São José school, which was situated on the wide avenue, Condé de Boa Vista. If more people came they could hold the meeting in the large patio that separates the school from the avenue.

The patio was to prove too small for the three thousand or so people of all conditions, secular and religious, who crammed in at nightfall. A small crowd at least as excited as the large crowd, filled the brightly lit balcony; actors, singers, journalists, some nuns, some priests. In a corner, back to the wall, stood Dom Helder, in scintillating mood, joining in the action. And it really was action already; this launching of the movement was not an academic session. It was, in the strict sense of the term, a demonstration.

A group of young actors introduced the aims of Action for Justice and Peace . . . 'Peace is our ideal. Not just any peace. Not a false peace. The true peace that Christ brought to all men of good will.'

1
A threat to humanity

1. Looking at the earth

How easy it is to find injustices everywhere; injustices of varying nature and varying degree, but injustices for all that.

In the underdeveloped countries these injustices—which are perhaps unknown elsewhere—affect millions of human beings, children of God, reducing them to a sub-human condition.

But what exactly do we mean by a 'sub-human condition'? Isn't it perhaps too strong a term, too tinged with demagogy? Not at all. There exists very often what could be called a heritage of poverty. It is common knowledge that poverty kills just as surely as the most bloody war. But poverty does more than kill, it leads to physical deformity (just think of Biafra), to psychological deformity (there are many cases of mental subnormality for which hunger is responsible), and to moral deformity (those who, through a situation of slavery, hidden but nonetheless real, are living without prospects and without hope, foundering in fatalism and reduced to a begging mentality).

But we must be careful! Injustices are not the monopoly of the underdeveloped countries. They exist in the developed countries too, just as much on the capitalist side as on the socialist.

In the capitalist world, even in the richest countries, there are underdeveloped strata which, in Canada, are beginning to be called 'grey belts'.

As we all know, President Lyndon Johnson declared war on poverty in the USA. According to him, thirty million North Americans were living under sub-human conditions. Although it is true that what are considered sub-human conditions in the developed countries are not quite the same as those in the underdeveloped countries, it is no less true that the gap between poverty and wealth in the rich countries provides some shocking contrasts.

In the socialist world, in practice (maybe the theory is different), the USSR, like Red China, does not accept pluralism within its society.

The struggle going on between the two great countries of the socialist bloc is illuminating in itself. Nevertheless both sides are striving equally to impose dialectical materialism and blind obedience. The climate is that of dictatorships, encouragement of informers and a reign of suspicion, of imposed self-criticism, of insecurity.

But injustices take on a completely different dimension when we look at the relations between the developed countries and the underdeveloped countries.

Twice the underdeveloped countries have tried to hold a dialogue with the developed countries, through UNCTAD.[1] The

[1] United Nations Conference on Trade and Development.

egoism and indifference in the two empires is alike, the capitalist empire with the USA at its head, and the socialist empire under the USSR.

Aid is certainly useful, but it will always be insufficient. The core of the problem will not be reached if no-one has the courage, which *Populorum Progressio* had,[2] to denounce the monstrous injustice according to which the present policy of international trade is organised.

Even the Pearson Report,[3] though it makes timid allusions to the problem of international trade, dwells much more on other points, such as the demographic explosion. Now, although there is a demographic problem, the Third World will never accept massive family planning, imposed from outside, nor will it allow the very complex problem of development to be reduced solely to the demographic plane.

[2] Encyclical letter of Pope Paul VI, translated as *The Great Social Problem*, London (Catholic Truth Society) 1967.
[3] *Partners in Development*, a report of the Commission on International Development.

This is really just a subterfuge, a pretext, another way of evading the central and overwhelming problem of injustice on a world-wide scale.

At the moment the developed world is proud and self-confident, with its nuclear bombs, and thinks it can afford to laugh at that giant with feet of clay, the under-developed world. But do the masters of the H-bomb really grasp the scope and conse-quences of the poverty bomb?

This is the situation of humanity at the beginning of the second development de-cade. If true development implies the de-velopment of *the whole man and of all men*, then there is not in fact a single truly developed country in the world.

But there is another unavoidable con-clusion which is still more serious, a con-clusion we must draw attention to because of its tragic consequences, and it is this. Look closely at the injustices in the under-developed countries, in the relations between the developed world and the un-derdeveloped world. You will find that everywhere the injustices are a form of violence. One can and must say that they are everywhere the basic violence, violence No. 1.

2. Violence attracts violence

No-one is born to be a slave. No-one seeks to suffer injustices, humiliations and restrictions. A human being condemned to a sub-human situation is like an animal —an ox or a donkey—wallowing in the mud.

Now the egoism of some privileged groups drives countless human beings into this sub-human condition, where they suffer restrictions, humiliations, injustices; without prospects, without hope, their condition is that of slaves.

This established violence, this violence No. 1, attracts violence No. 2, revolt, either of the oppressed themselves or of youth, firmly resolved to battle for a more just and human world.

Certainly there are, from continent to continent, from country to country, from city to city, variations, differences, degrees, nuances, in violence No. 2, but generally in the world today the oppressed are opening their eyes.

The authorities and the privileged are alarmed by the presence of agents coming from outside whom they call 'subversive elements', 'agitators', 'communists'.

Sometimes they are indeed people committed to an ideology of the extreme left who are fighting for the liberation of the oppressed and have opted for armed violence. At other times they are people moved by religious feeling, who can no longer tolerate religion interpreted and lived as an opium for the masses, as an alien and alienating force, but want to see it at the service of the human development of those who are imprisoned in a sub-human condition.

The authorities and the privileged lump the two groups together. For them, those who, in the name of their religion (whether they are clergy or laity), are working for fundamental reforms, for a change in structures, have abandoned religion for politics, are foundering in leftism or, at the very least, are innocents preparing the way for communism.

There are two main counter-arguments to this attitude. The authorities and the privileged pretend to believe that without the presence of 'agitators', the oppressed masses would remain with their eyes closed, passive and immobile.

Today, with all the means of transport and social communication available (including the transistor radio), it is ridiculous to think that one can prevent the circulation of ideas or the spread of information.

And secondly, monolithic and obsessional anti-communism is responsible for many absurdities. The prime one is maintaining injustices because tackling them 'might open the door to communism'.

In those places where the oppressed masses have an opportunity for direct action they engage in more or less thoroughgoing, bitter and prolonged agitation. When the masses have fallen into a kind of fatalism for lack of hope, or when a too violent reaction cows them for an instant, then it is the young who rise.

The young no longer have the patience to wait for the privileged to discard their privileges. The young very often see governments too tied to the privileged classes. The young are losing confidence in the churches, which affirm beautiful principles —great texts, remarkable conclusions—but without ever deciding, at least so far, to translate them into real life.

The young then are turning more and more to radical action and violence.

In some places the young are the force of idealism, fire, hunger for justice, thirst for authenticity. In others, with the same enthusiasm, they adopt extremist ideologies and prepare for 'guerilla warfare' in town or country.

If there is some corner of the world which has remained peaceful, but with a peace based on injustices—the peace of a swamp with rotten matter fermenting in its depths —we may be sure that that peace is false.

Violence attracts violence. Let us repeat fearlessly and ceaselessly: injustices bring revolt, either from the oppressed or from the young, determined to fight for a more just and more human world.

3. And then comes repression

When conflict comes out into the streets, when violence No. 2 tries to resist violence No. 1, the authorities consider themselves obliged to preserve or re-establish public order, even if this means using force; this is violence No. 3. Sometimes they go even further, and this is becoming increasingly common: in order to obtain information, which may indeed be important to public security, the logic of violence leads them to use moral and physical torture—as though any information extracted through torture deserved the slightest attention!

In the developed countries there are very often protests against the torture used in underdeveloped countries. The intentions are very generous and the results often very good. It is a liberating moral pressure:

governments do not like to appear despotic or backward in the eyes of the world.

But no developed country need harbour any illusions: everywhere violence will come, everywhere the protest of the oppressed or of youth, confronted with injustices, will gain ground; everywhere it will manage to create a feeling of panic in the world of the oppressors.

Is it or is it not true that some universities in the rich countries—to confront the excesses of youthful protest (taking over buildings, burning of buildings, bloody battles)—have asked for and obtained special powers from the government? There are cases in which the rector will now be able to decree a state of emergency.

How is it that the psychologists, sociologists and educators did not foresee the bitterness of the young, their growing revolt, their despair? Could one not hope that the youth explosion would have been predicted, foreseen and avoided, that it would have been possible to face up to everything that is true and just in the agitation of the young, even the demands exploited by professional activists? What a bad example to appeal to violence and force!. Tomorrow, if protest spreads, the governments will already have received suggestions from the universities themselves. . . .

Who does not remember that even peoples of a high cultural level have sunk into a dictatorship at a troubled moment in their national life? And even among these peoples of a high cultural level, incredible atrocities have been witnessed, under the eternal pretext of obtaining information.

Psychological warfare—employed both by the extreme left and the extreme right, and by democratic regimes who are beginning to see protest increasing—considers itself scientific.

It is the old Inquisition, with the technology of the nuclear and space travel age at its service.

Let us have the honesty to admit, in the light of the past and, perhaps, here and there, in the light of some typical reactions, that violence No. 3—governmental repression, under the pretext of safeguarding public order, national security, the free world—is not a monopoly of the under-developed countries.

There is not a country in the world which is in no danger of falling into the throes of violence.

4. A real threat

Is there a real danger of seeing the injustices in the world getting worse? What is one to think of the efforts of the developed countries to deal with the underdevelopment and poverty of the poor countries? What is one to think of the efforts of the developed countries to eliminate the underdeveloped strata in their own lands?

In the underdeveloped countries, since the basic reforms, the changes in socio-economic, political and cultural structures, only exist on paper, the same conclusion will always be reached: the rich are getting richer, the poor poorer.

The most well-known case of 'war against poverty' in a developed country is the United States. The Vietnam war has absorbed the peaceful war which was trying to wrest thirty million North Americans from a sub-human condition.

Today it is not easy to predict the exact course of the Vietnam affair, its consequences for the life of the United States in general and, in particular, for the millions of 'poor' living among the citizens of the richest country in the world. . . .

No clear signs of change are to be seen in the structures of any developed country in the capitalist camp (the socialist camp also has grave problems, as will one day be seen).

The rich will accept talk of aid: for those of their own country and even for the Third World. But it is not done to talk too much about justice, rights, structural changes. . . .

UNCTAD constitutes the great unknown. What is one to think of discussion involving 1% or 2% of the gross national product—which in itself demonstrates a total incomprehension of the very essence of the problem of relations between the developed world and the underdeveloped world. Aid is necessary, but not enough. Until someone has the courage and intelligence to undertake a complete revision of international trade policy, the poor countries will continue to get poorer and to enrich the wealthy countries more and more.

But the reaction of the oppressed also shows clear signs of becoming sharper. It is impossible to keep them enclosed, out of circulation. It suffices to know what is happening in the world. The oppressed of yesterday, the downtrodden, the timid, are opening their eyes, becoming aware, taking courage.

And the young are there. It is easy to say that after their student days are over the young critics will tend to calm down, settle down, become bourgeois. But there are young people preparing themselves to keep the flame alive.

The world is heading for trouble, protest, violence, coming from the oppressed and the young.

Who has any illusions about the stepping up of governmental reactions? We need only consider how many countries have submitted in our time to extra-constitutional governments or dictatorships. Look at the map and count the number of countries in the hands of the military.

Thus, the inescapable conclusion is that there is a real threat of an escalation of violence, of seeing the world fall into a spiral of violence.

2
A valid solution

1. Is armed violence the only solution?

When humanity is under the threat of being engulfed in violence and hatred, we have no right to comfort ourselves with illusions, to reassure ourselves with pseudo-solutions, whose main drawback is to distract our attention from the difficult and daring solutions which are perhaps the true ones.

Let us have the courage to ask ourselves: does not non-violent action serve as a tranquilliser? Apart from armed violence, has an underdeveloped country any chance of tearing itself out of underdevelopment, or have the underdeveloped strata of a rich country any chance of reaching the general standard of national development?

As a first attempt at a reply, let us try to examine the real possibilities of armed violence. There are voices which tell us that the solution lies in making more Vietnams. It is important, then, to seek the truth about Vietnam, especially as regards the situation of the people.

In broad terms, the situation can be summed up as follows: Vietnam is a field on which the capitalist empire and the socialist empire are locked in battle.

It will perhaps appear unjust to place on an equal footing the North American soldier and the Vietnamese boy fighting in the ranks of the National Liberation Front, Vietnamese who wish, purely and simply, to defend their country and ultimately attain the right to live in peace. And among these, there will doubtless be also Buddhists and Catholics, the purest and sincerest.

But when it is known that the war in Vietnam is costing the United States twenty-seven thousand million dollars a year, i.e. seventy-four million dollars a day; when we know that already more bombs have been dropped on North Vietnam than on Germany and her satellites during the second world war; when one listens, in the American senate, to voices revealing that each Vietcong killed costs the United States three hundred and fifty dollars, it becomes evident that, however heroic the heroism of Vietnam, the American victory would have been total and certain if another empire had not been spending similar sums and supplying equally modern and deadly weapons. And the American leaders already acknowledge the practical impossibility of a victory in Vietnam.

One could continue to call absurd the comparison between the resources employed by the Americans to dominate and those utilised by the National Liberation Front to defend the country. Here we have the saddest and gravest lesson of the Vietnamese war: the Front, while accepting and desiring tacit alliances at the moment of battle against the common enemy, has a political philosophy imposed on it by the empire which finances it which includes dialectical materialism, blind obedience to the Party and all the methods of insecurity, encouragement of informers and periodic purges inherent in dictatorships of left or right.

Thich Nhat Hanh, in *Vietnam: the Lotus in the sea of fire*,[1] proclaims the real situation of Vietnam, which is, no one will deny, a prefiguration of the fate of any underdeveloped country should it have the misfortune to be transformed into a battle-field between empires which scarcely bother to conceal, under ideological pretexts, objectives of political prestige and the advantages resulting from it for their economic war.

Thich Nhat Hanh concludes that what is happening in Vietnam is a war between the United States and the Chinese People's Republic, even though the latter do not have troops in Vietnam.

It is not easy to predict what will be the decisive factor in the Vietnam war. It seems clear that even a first-rate power

[1] London (SCM Press) 1967.

cannot defeat guerillas if it cannot count on the support of the population. But it seems just as clear that guerilla war only tackles the warlike power with great force when it has another great power behind it.

This is to say that the liberation of Vietnam (and of the countries which will suffer the same fate) is very relative: either the people continue to be a satellite in the capitalist orbit, or they are condemned to revolve as a satellite in the socialist orbit.

2. Gandhi, failure or prophet?

If one takes Gandhi as the prototype of the leader of active and courageous non-violence, now is the time to ask: 'Gandhi, where is thy victory?'

In the short term, Gandhi seems to have failed. What, truly, are the prospects for his teaching, both in the underdeveloped countries and in the developed countries?

Here, in our opinion, are the Gandhian possibilities in the Third World. For truth and liberating moral pressure to be a real alternative to armed revolution, it seems essential that the established regime should have a minimum of respect for the rights of man, notably for freedom of expression. It is furthermore necessary that no totalitarian methods should be established to falsify truth, and no physical or moral tortures.

If a member of the movement, acting in agreement with the principles and methods of peaceful violence, is put in prison, one of the resources of the movement should be to gather dozens, hundreds, thousands of fellow members who would also agree to give themselves up at the same time at the gates of the prison, declaring their solidarity with their outraged brother. This would clearly cause a sensation. And through the accounts of the newspapers, radio and television, and through the press agencies, the movement would obtain national and international recognition.

But, in the underdeveloped countries, authoritarian regimes easily take control under the pretext of safeguarding 'the social order' from attack by subversive elements or communists. Moreover, the press, radio and television only transmits what favours the regime and it is obvious that it will not venture to reflect liberating moral pressure.

Worse still: the communications media find themselves obliged to spread lies or distortions of the facts, directly and sometimes officially communicated by the information services.

Informers are encouraged. Moral and physical torture is employed as a scientific method of wresting confessions from the 'subversive' elements, or those supposed to be such. Instead of innocence being presumed until a crime is proved, the crime is presumed, and even if the suspect is freed, through total lack of evidence against him and through the presence of indisputable evidence in his favour, no open and frank acknowledgment of the error committed is ever obtained.

How can moral pressure be brought into action in order to stir consciences as a preliminary condition for a change of structures—if access to the newspapers and magazines, to radio and television, is forbidden, without formal prohibition, but by secret but effective order, in the name of national security? How can liberating moral pressure be brought into action if meetings and gatherings are prohibited in public places, and if conferences behind closed doors draw suspicion both on the speakers and the participants?

Furthermore, one of the most terrible weapons of the authoritarian regimes is to spare the great leader and seize the humble collaborators, who are without inner assurance, without moral resistance, insufficiently prepared to be able to face complex, malicious and treacherous interrogation.

When Gandhi went on a hunger strike, the whole world was grieved and there was no empire, however powerful, capable of resisting the moral pressure which arose from the four corners of the earth. But let us suppose that the established regime had left Gandhi without a voice, had placed his closest and dearest collaborators in prison, that it had spread about them the worst slanders (for example that they informed against their comrades, that they were afraid and had admitted their participation in subversive movements, that they abandoned Satyagraha . . .) what would the apostle of non-violence have been able to do?

One might think of having recourse to leaflets and manifestos: but those who handed them out would be placed in prison and tortured as dangerous agitators, those who printed or stencilled them would be beaten and their machines destroyed.

It is obvious that, among the simple people and those who are just beginning to become aware of things, the news of prisons and above all of tortures leads to fear and flight from the Movement. Use the pulpit? Surely priests acting in this way would not be understood by the majority of the faithful, who would reproach them with straying from their evangelical mission and accuse them of engaging in politics.

It is clear that anyone who, in proclaiming the Gospel, demands justice as condition of peace, risks imprisonment; if he is a foreigner, he will be expelled.

More serious still for the priest than being put in prison is *not* being put in prison, but seeing in prison all around him militant laymen who have simply echoed the evangelical message.

In such a climate, is it not obvious that the young above all are going to abandon the violence of the peace-lovers, go underground and try to prepare for armed revolution?

Now we repeat again and again: if Vietnam proves that even a first-class power cannot defeat guerillas if it does not have the support of the local population, it also proves that the greatest heroism in the world cannot stand up to a first-class power except when it can count on another supporting it from behind. Do not let us deceive ourselves. The socialist empires, whether of Soviet or Chinese allegiance, are just as cold and insensible as the capitalist empires towards the underdeveloped countries' hope for total development. The capitalist empires, with their affirmations of sacrifice for the free world, of defence of private enterprise, of safeguarding order from subversion and chaos, are in fact defending their political prestige and the economic interests arising from it; they are indeed at the service of economic power and the international trusts. The socialist empires for their part are hard and intransigent, they do not allow pluralism, they impose dialectical materialism, demand blind obedience to the party, set up a regime of total and permanent insecurity and fear, just like the fascist dictatorships of the extreme right.

What would Gandhi say, what would he advise the Third World to do, faced with the situation of humanity one hundred years after his birth?

But has Gandhi's doctrine perhaps a greater chance in the developed countries? Perhaps it is precisely there that the change of structures should begin without which the poor countries will never escape from their poverty. If not, there will never be respect for the human person, nor climate of freedom, nor any scope for a moral action which proves its efficacy—not with the objects of mere reformism, but to obtain profound and rapid changes which alone would render the appeal to armed revolution unnecessary.

But here too grave doubts arise. The

influence of the universities on public opinion, especially that of the great and powerful universities, those of the developed countries, is considerable. Now we are in process of witnessing strange and dangerous reactions in the very heart of these universities: to face up to student protest and—let us admit it—the excesses, abuses and petty terror which accompany it, the universities, which have a universal responsibility, have not yet found a method equal to their mission of wisdom, and they appeal for discretionary powers: a terrible example and dangerous precedent, in that tomorrow a new dictatorship could be installed. To what point can this be explained by the bonds linking these universities, either directly with the public powers, or indirectly with the economic powers through the intermediary of the foundations that subsidise them?

The means of social communication represent an immense force, and one until very recently unknown in such proportions. But in the underdeveloped countries they are a giant with feet of clay, given the facility with which they can be manipulated by the state.

In the developed countries of the capitalist world, the mass media are beginning to become businesses, and huge businesses at that. The freedom of journalists is now becoming, in most cases, a very relative thing: it ends where the interests of the business begin. When independent and courageous newspapers exist they are destroyed, as happened in Italy with *L'Avvenire dell'Italia*.

In socialist areas, it is enough to recall that the means of social communication are the monopoly of the party.

Religions, in capitalist areas, run a very grave risk of being caught up in the system. They are courageous in broadcasting beautiful principles, but without sufficient energy to carry them through, for the very reason—though perhaps an unconscious one—that they will be themselves affected by the process of incorporation.

In socialist areas, religions are reduced to alien and alienating forces, through the absolute prohibition made on them to undertake any sort of involvement in the socio-economic field, in the direction of human development.

Would there be some hope in a dialogue between political leaders, young managers and young leaders of the workers? It is unnecessary to point out the practical difficulties which would arise from a dialogue capable of leading to changes in depth of the present shape of international trade policy, the heart of the fundamental injustice between developed and underdeveloped worlds.

Must we then conclude that in the developed countries the chances of Gandhi and of the movements inspired by him and his example are so small, if not non-existent?

No! Time is working for Gandhi. Soon, he will be acknowledged as a prophet. And here are the main reasons why. Ultimately, man will manage to convince himself of the absurdity of war. World wars, since the discovery of nuclear energy, are plain suicide. Local wars—Vietnam is there to prove it—take just as heavy a toll in human lives, in money and in prestige as world wars.

Everywhere, as well as an inert majority

and an extreme left and extreme right who clash with one another in a shifting balance of violence and hatred, there are minorities who are well aware that violence is not the real answer to violence; that, if violence is met by violence, the world will fall into a spiral of violence; that the only true answer to violence is to have the courage to face the injustices which constitute violence No. 1.

The privileged and the authorities will come to understand that common sense obliges one to choose between bloody and armed violence, on the one hand, and on the other the violence of the peaceful: liberating moral pressure.

To those who think that the authorities and the privileged will never yield to the violence of the peaceful—which will not be satisfied with minor reforms, but demands definite changes in unjust and inhuman structures—it suffices to recall that their children are very often on the side of justice and that these young people are a powerful voice in support of the demand for a more united and human world.

3
Action for Justice and Peace

1. Objectives and outlook

Action for Justice and Peace is self-explanatory: its aims are announced in its name:

—*Action*: not just speculation, theory, discussion, contemplation;
—*Justice*: there are injustices everywhere; everywhere there is need for justice;
—*Peace*: justice is the condition for peace, the path, the way. It is only through justice that a true and lasting peace will be achieved.

All those who, all over the world, hunger and thirst after justice, are invited to march together:

—*the oppressed* who suffer injustice, those of the underdeveloped countries, and also those in the underdeveloped strata of the rich countries;

—*those who* belong to the privileged classes of the poor countries or the rich classes of the rich countries but *no longer accept injustice* and acknowledge it to be violence No. 1;

—*the technologists*, who are best placed to understand the gravity of the ever-widening gulf between the developed world and the underdeveloped world and who, by nature and by profession, prefer liberating moral pressure to bloody violence;

—*those who*, having opted for bloody and armed violence, *are beginning to wonder whether the violence of the pacifists is not the true solution*;

—*those who* still are, or who were until yesterday, the authorities, and who have answered violence with violence (indeed even with torture), but who now *understand the urgency of the violence of the pacifists in demanding justice* without falling into armed violence and hatred.

All those who, all over the world, hunger and thirst after justice and accept the invitation to march together in the Action for Justice and Peace must know:

—that the AJP is not and never will be a political party;

—that it does not belong in any way to one man, one party, one country, one culture or one religion;

—that it is a gathering of men of good will convinced that only the roads of justice and love lead to true peace, who are resolved to exercise liberating moral pressure to obtain justice and help humanity to free itself from hatred and chaos.

Within his own religion, each person will discover the necessary impulse to give himself entirely to justice as condition of peace.

Alongside the development of Action for Justice and Peace, it will one day be necessary to collect from the sacred books of all the religions the exhortations, precepts and prayers which speak about peace and justice, and similarly the examples of the great models in the various religions. For some religions the word 'justice' always presupposes such virtues, and is in fact a synonym for holiness.

As for peace, it is well-known that there can be instances of false peace, with the same deceptive beauty as stagnant marshes in moonlight. The peace which speaks to us, which moves us, for which we are prepared to give our lives, presupposes that the rights of all are fully respected: the rights of God and the rights of men. Not just the rights of some men, a privileged few, to the detriment of many others: the rights of each man and of all men.

Very vague? Too vague? God, who loves peace and knows that it is the fruit of justice, will help men of good will. His Spirit will breathe over the earth as he breathed over the waters at the beginning of creation.

What seems vague will become definite. What seems obscure will become clear. And the movement which seems to be without a leader, without a guide, will be led directly by the Lord.

2. Beyond the barriers

Is it possible to envisage a world movement when there are so many barriers, of so many different kinds, so many divisions between men, so many obstacles which often appear insuperable?

Without being blind to the problems created by the differences in race, language, country and religion; without forgetting hatred, struggles, coldness and egoism, is it a dream or an illusion to think that there are, everywhere, people who have made up their minds to demand, in a peaceful but resolute way, justice as condition of peace?

Whatever the colour of your skin, the shape of your lips or your nose, whatever your height, you are neither a sub-man nor a superman; you are a human creature. You have a head, a heart, hopes, dreams. More important still: the creator and Father has a whole plan of human fulfilment which involves you.

If you belong to a tribe, a family, a race, you belong too to the human family. The injustices you encounter in your own environment exist everywhere.

If you have a special love for your race, for your people, come and join all those who are resolved to build a more united and human world. Whatever your language, little known or well known, primitive or rich—we shall be able to understand you.

A look, a smile, gestures of peace and friendship, attention and delicacy, these are the universal language, capable of demonstrating that we are much closer to one another than we imagined. Everywhere kindness touches, injustice wounds, peace is an ideal.

Keep your language. Love its sounds, its modulation, its rhythm. But try to march together with men of different languages, remote from your own, who wish like you for a more just and human world.

Whatever your country—a little clan in the midst of enemy tribes or a nation extending its power—know that, in your own land, whoever truly possesses the spirit of Action for Justice and Peace will not feel a stranger.

It is true that each of us has his own country. But, while respecting and loving the country in which God caused us to be born, having special ties with our country-men, it is still possible to feel above all a man among men, a brother among brothers.

Do you understand this argument? You will say yes, but you will think that men think and act very differently. There are frontiers, customs posts, barriers, the distances, the egoism crying to the other that he is a stranger.

Come and help to build together a world in which all men will recognise and love one another as brothers!

Whatever your religion, try to demand that, instead of separating men, it helps to unite them.

War of religions! Is this not the tragedy to end all tragedies, a contradiction in terms, an absurdity! God is Love. Religion must gather men, draw them together.

In the teachings of your faith, what are the principles, the directives which call for justice and peace?

If your life has taken you far from

religious practice or even from faith, perhaps you still love truth. Perhaps you are capable of suffering for justice. Then you will be able to help a great deal and serve as an example in difficult times!

Beyond the barriers let us unite! If existing minorities—and there are minorities within all races, languages, countries and religions—can come together in Action for Justice and Peace, we shall have the right to hope.

3. Practical points

Action for Justice and Peace wishes to exercise liberating moral pressure to help, in a peaceful but effective way:
—to change the socio-economic, political and cultural structures of the underdeveloped countries;
—to induce the developed countries to integrate their underdeveloped strata and to revise radically the international policies governing trade with the underdeveloped countries.

A fundamental point is documentation.

AJP must be well-informed: its moral force will be won by the seriousness, accuracy and objectivity of its statements. Obviously arguments will always be possible, but individuals and organisations must be able to take seriously the reports, analyses and proposals of AJP.

Here are some suggestions for basic documentation on underdeveloped countries:

—with regard to Latin America, the phrase 'internal colonialism' is used in this continent to refer to those groups of privileged people whose wealth is based on the poverty of millions of their own fellow-countrymen.

This raises the following questions:

—What is the truth about this phenomenon of internal colonialism in Latin America? If the thesis is correct, how can it be supported?

—Are Africa and Asia similarly suffering from this internal colonialism, or is the African and Asian situation in this respect totally different?

—The developed countries have difficulty in understanding the expression 'sub-human situation'. To bring it home to them, what are the points to concentrate on, the truest and most striking aspects? Housing conditions? Quantity and quality of food? Scarcity of clothing? The absence of a basic educational system? The lack of basic guarantees for working conditions? The lack of prospects and hope? The condition of de facto slavery?

And now the same suggestions directed at the underdeveloped strata of the rich countries:

—Is it true that even the richest countries have their 'grey belts', their underdeveloped strata? How can this be demonstrated?

—It is likely that there is a real difference between the underdevelopment of the poor countries and the underdevelopment of the rich countries, but it is also likely that the gap between rich and poor, within the rich countries, is shocking. How can we make people see and feel this?

Here are some suggestions connected with the necessary documentation on the relations between the developed and underdeveloped countries:

—In August 1968, the prime minister of Jamaica paid a visit to Canada. According to a Canadian newspaper[1] he said then that his country, to buy a Canadian tractor, had to pay in 1966 the equivalent of 680 tons of sugar; in 1968, for the same Canadian tractor, the price was the equivalent of 3,500 tons of sugar. How can this grave situation of the declining prices of primary products be translated into terms corresponding to the problem of each country of the Third World?

—In the course of the last fifteen years, the investments in Latin America coming from the United States have risen to 3,800,000,000 dollars. During the same period, the revenue from the investments repatriated to the United States has risen to 11,300,000,000 dollars.[2]

Information such as this is of importance as it is necessary as basis for studies and dis-

[1] *Le Devoir*, 12.8.1968.

[2] *Le Monde*, Paris, 24.10.1968, quoted by the 'Memorandum on Canada's foreign policy towards Latin America' (reference 11), submitted to the Canadian Government by a Group of Oblate Missionaries of Canada (8844 Est, Notre Dame, Montreal 430).

cussions. It exists in the Reports of the United Nations Conference on Trade and Development (UNCTAD). You certainly know that the underdeveloped countries at Geneva and at New Delhi have made a remarkable effort to show that in the relations between the developed and the underdeveloped worlds, aid is necessary but insufficient.

Until someone has the courage to undertake a thorough revision of international trade policies, the poor countries will continue to feed the wealth of the rich countries with their blood.[3]

Another type of information is connected with physical violence, either on the part of the oppressed themselves or on the part of the young, both in the underdeveloped

[3] Your group should try to obtain the relevant UNCTAD reports. A selection of these is available in Britain from Her Majesty's Stationery Office and in the USA from The Bookshop, United Nations Headquarters, New York NY 10017. For detailed information write to UNCTAD, Information Service, United Nations Office, Palais des Nations, Geneva, Switzerland.

countries and in the poor areas of the rich countries.

What are we to make of the impatience of those who go over to radical action and armed violence? Not that we want to join them—our choice has already been made for Action for Justice and Peace—nor is it just idle curiosity. It is a human interest, coupled with respect for those who, in conscience, have made a different choice but one which is no less devoted to the cause of justice.

Action for Justice and Peace has taken it upon itself to study any violent reaction by the authorities under the pretext of safeguarding public order. It undertakes in particular to protest each time it finds out for certain that torture is employed as a 'scientific' method of extracting information, even when this information may be important or crucial to national security.

Who is going to find this information? Who? How? When? Where? Can one speak in the name of Action for Justice and Peace? Where does it operate? Who has the right to accept or authorise its members? Is the movement recognised? Is there not the risk of seeing someone exploit the movement for his own ends?

One cannot create a movement of trust where distrust prevails. We use this principle as point of departure: everywhere there are minorities capable of understanding Action for Justice and Peace and adopting it as a workshop for study and action. Let us call these minorities the *Abrahamic minorities*, because, like Abraham, we are hoping against all hope.

Do you think you are alone? Look around you. Talk to your friends. Talk to people in your house, in your neighbourhood, at your school, at your work, with your leisure companions. You will be surprised to discover that your 'Abrahamic minority' already exists. And you were unaware of it.

A plan of study and action should be set up at once. Go over again the list of information to be obtained. Try to complete it.

Your Abrahamic minority will perhaps need a clear mind, someone of experience, capable of guiding the first steps, and getting studies and action under way. This 'someone' already exists: all you have to do is find him.

Encourage the birth of other Abrahamic minorities in your town, in your area, in your country. It is obvious that a number of Abrahamic minorities should help one another.

These are the preliminary steps. But ultimately, what must the AJP do and how must it act if it hopes to attain its very important and very difficult objectives?

The Abrahamic minorities must discover the means of making different sorts of contacts:

With the leaders of the privileged classes, on condition that the group possesses someone with an authoritative character who is capable of presenting the hardest truths in the most authentic charity;

With the leaders of the various religions. The Catholics of Latin America, at Medellin (Colombia) and the Protestants at Uppsala (Sweden) reached very grave conclusions about injustices. Together, Catholics and Protestants have signed the great text of Beirut about justice on a world scale.

There must be similar movements within the other religions. The time has come when each religion must rediscover, in its sacred texts, the truths capable of encouraging the human development of the outcasts of the modern world and of arousing the consciences of the rich.

Who will manage to make the universities examine the UNCTAD reports in depth? If they have no value, they should be torn up. If they are true, then it is terribly serious, since they denounce injustice on a global scale.

Who will manage to get the universities to discover new models of development, which depend neither on the capitalist nor on the socialist empires? Perhaps the way to a solution is through a socialisation which truly assures the development of the whole man and of all men. . . .

Is one justified in expecting, in the universities of the developed countries, institutes of study and research specialising in the problems of the Third World?

The press, radio and television deserve particular attention. It is well known that economic power is making its presence strongly felt in this field. Abrahamic minorities among the reporters working in the newspapers, the weeklies, the radio and television companies, or in the press agencies, will obviously be of very particular significance and their influence will be exceptional.

Why not attempt dialogue with the military? When it comes down to it, under the helmet there is a man, a brother in humanity. And it is evident that within the armed forces there are Abrahamic minorities to be aroused, encouraged, rallied to Action for Justice and Peace.

And politicians? One must try to approach them, with both the innocence of the dove and the cunning of the serpent. . . .

Sometimes, for a certain time, the conditions of a country do not offer the minimum possibility of action. At such times one studies, suffers, waits. The responsibility of those countries where freedom still exists then becomes even greater.

On the international plane there are organisations which arouse the hopes of AJP.

Christians now have a Pontifical Commission for *Justice and Peace* and a World Council of Churches, both earnestly concerned with opening roads of justice and obtaining peace. What are the analogous movements in other religions?

When will the great religions of the world decide to devote all their moral force to demanding justice as condition of peace?

Will an organisation such as UNESCO have the necessary independence, the moral force and the interest sufficient to unite the universities of North and South, of the capitalist countries and the socialist countries, for the construction of a more just and human world?

It is vital for the developed countries to come to understand that, without a change

73

of structures at home, a change of structures in the underdeveloped countries is impossible.

If these suggestions seem indefinite and vague, do some research and set your imagination to work. We have presented some practical ways of acting: it is for the Abrahamic minorities of today and of tomorrow to go further, to say and above all to do the rest, always faithful to the paths of justice and love, as condition of peace.

4. A world movement

Let us hope against all hope, and imagine that the Abrahamic minorities will multiply on the five continents and on the seven seas. Whom then to speak to? Whom to turn to? Whom to consult? At all costs the erroneous idea must be avoided that Action for Justice and Peace is bound to any particular country, any particular language, any particular religion. No Abrahamic minority has accounts to render to any authority.

But it is easy to understand that, at first,

for some, it is convenient, or almost necessary, to orientate oneself, to have a point of reference, an information centre, an exchange centre.

Wherever possible, a circular will be sent regularly to those Abrahamic minorities whose addresses are known, as an attempt to pool initiatives, experiences and suggestions.

The moral force of Action for Justice and Peace will be born of communication between the Abrahamic minorities from the different towns, different countries, different continents.

When the Abrahamic minorities of the Third World feel themselves truly in solidarity and, above all, when they meet fraternal echoes coming to them from the developed countries, humanity will have taken a step towards peace.

The Spirit breathes where it will. It is perfectly possible for Abrahamic minorities to emerge in North and South, East and West. Even under totalitarian regimes the idea of

Action for Justice and Peace will be able to flourish.

Is pluralism possible within Action for Justice and Peace? Not only possible, but desirable. Safeguarded by the essence of the movement, defined by its name, its ideal will be unity but not uniformity, variety in unity.

The movement would have no deep vitality if it took the same form in Brazil as in France, in the Indies as in the United States, in the Cameroons as in Australia. Each race, each language, each religion must leave its own mark on the movement.

Is there room for conflict? Obviously. If Action for Justice and Peace does not set itself up as a sign of contradiction, if it does not provoke disquiet, if it does not sow doubts, if it does not arouse great devotion and provoke hatred, then it is preparing its own funeral.

It does not claim to be *the* solution. It hopes to help men at a time when all of us are groping for a way out.

And as for the languages: what are the official languages for correspondence? I say any one. There is always someone to help understand. And the heart will guess the rest. The important thing is to get started. Time is pressing. We are hundreds of years behind, and all of us bear direct responsibility for the sin of omission.

5. Appeal to youth

Young people, my friends, my brothers.

Perhaps I am making a mistake or am suffering under an illusion: but I continue to be fascinated by the youth of today. Many of my hopes for a more just and human world find their roots and their support in the young.

I continue to think, as at Manchester,[4] in England, that the young no longer tolerate the seven capital sins of the modern world: *racialism, colonialism, war, paternalism, pharisaism, alienation and fear.*

You cannot imagine how many letters I receive telling terrible tales about the young of today. Over against the seven

[4] Speech to the Congress of the British Student Christian Movement, 'Response to Crisis', April 1969.

capital sins you are fighting, they emphasise the seven capital sins into which you are said to fall: snobbery, mental laziness, protest, drugs, sex, compromise and atheism.

They talk about your snobbery, because of your clothes, your music, your language, your reactions: people forget that every generation has its own style—it suffices to glance through an old family album. . . .

Mental laziness? You do not accept teaching which is dry as dust, out of date and remote from life, which the university tries to instil into you. The adults should have a go at discussing with you the real and terrible human problems of our time! . . .

How can you not protest when you have to break through a shell of prejudices and to break down inhuman and reactionary structures? It is true that you often take your protest too far and that in doing so you invade your schools, take them over and sometimes ransack them. It is a pity that the universities—crammed as they are with psychologists, sociologists and educators—have shown themselves incapable of foreseeing your revolt while it was taking shape, and that they do not manage to engage in dialogue with you. Some only discover the appeal to force, when the solution demands understanding and love. In demanding or in accepting special powers such as that of declaring a state of emergency, they offer a sad and terrible lesson to governments, which are already too inclined to dictatorships in law or in fact.

As for drugs and narcotics: without doubt you yourselves, the young, are already convinced that drugs are only a false hope, whose price in terms of health, vitality and creativity is too heavy. Doubtless you yourselves think already of snatching your colleagues, your friends, your brothers out of this tragic snare, laid by soulless mercenaries, experts in commercialising vice, even at the cost of your lives. But it is a pity that the adults do not ask themselves what lies at the basis of the despair and bitterness which drives the young to this attempt at evasion. Those who condemn the young are very often incapable of thinking that perhaps their egoism, their lack of understanding and openness are directly connected with the drug invasion.

In what period has sex not exercised its powerful attractions? Certainly you yourselves—more simple, more authentic, more direct—feel the necessity to investigate the mystery of love which, though it very often involves sex, is by no means reduced to the call of the flesh. Too much talk is made of free love. But what is love really, and when can one talk of freedom?

Compromise? Here lies a real danger. To the degree in which the compromise all around you is broad and tempting, the struggle to be undertaken is more arduous. And compromise is a siren ready to seduce you.

Your position with regard to religion and God depends to a great extent on our attitude and our response to life. When you meet people who are trying to live a religion which refuses to be an opium of the masses, an alien and alienating force; when you meet people for whom the love of God involves human love, your atheism will give way to respect, to sympathy—who knows?—to faith.

And now I have a question to ask you,

precisely because I know that we have all a world in common, even if you disagree with me and consider me a dreamer and a fool.

You have heard my appeal. The important thing now is not to agree with its positions, but to discuss them. I have no need to ask you for sincerity (you abhor hypocrisy and lies). I ask you to challenge facts with facts, arguments with arguments. I ask you to bring new points of view or new perspectives.

If I know you as well as I think I do, we are in agreement on our way of looking at this world which is groaning with injustices. And injustice is for you violence No. 1.

You will agree in recognising that, in general, youth is losing patience and slipping into radical action and armed violence.

You also agree that the governments are ready to react in a brutal way. And they have no scruples, even when it comes to torture. Your doubt—or the doubt of many of you—bears on the following point: is non-violence feasible, even in a positive and demanding movement such as Action for Justice and Peace?

What separates us? We are united in our aims: we wish for a more just and human world. You think perhaps that only armed violence will have the power to shake and demolish the inhuman structures which create slaves.

If I joyfully spend the rest of my life, of my powers, of my energies in demanding justice, but without hatred, without armed violence, through liberating moral pressure, through truth and love, it is because I am convinced that only love is constructive and strong.

I know your sincerity and I respect your choice. Leave no-one indifferent around you. Provoke discussions. Your youth must force people to think and take up a position: let it be uncomfortable, like truth, demanding, like justice.

Help Action for Justice and Peace: support it, challenge it, discuss it. You may be surprised to find yourselves helping the Abrahamic minorities, enabling them to assert themselves and to act.

This is my appeal. Bring me your warmth and your friendship. With you I must remain young in soul, keep the hope and love I need to help all men, our brothers.